GERANIUM

A Comedy in One Act

By Arnold Ridley

Copyright © 1954 Arnold Ridley
All Rights Reserved

GERANIUM is fully protected under the copyright laws of the British Commonwealth, including Canada, the United States of America, and all other countries of the Copyright Union. All rights, including professional and amateur stage productions, recitation, lecturing, public reading, motion picture, radio broadcasting, television, online/digital production, and the rights of translation into foreign languages are strictly reserved.

ISBN 978-0-573-13378-7

concordtheatricals.co.uk
concordtheatricals.com

FOR AMATEUR PRODUCTION ENQUIRIES

UNITED KINGDOM AND WORLD
EXCLUDING NORTH AMERICA
licensing@concordtheatricals.co.uk
020-7054-7298

Each title is subject to availability from Concord Theatricals,
depending upon country of performance.

CAUTION: Professional and amateur producers are hereby warned that *GERANIUM* is subject to a licensing fee. The purchase, renting, lending or use of this book does not constitute a licence to perform this title(s), which licence must be obtained from the appropriate agent prior to any performance. Performance of this title(s) without a licence is a violation of copyright law and may subject the producer and/or presenter of such performances to penalties. Both amateurs and professionals considering a production are strongly advised to apply to the appropriate agent before starting rehearsals, advertising, or booking a theatre. A licensing fee must be paid whether the title is presented for charity or gain and whether or not admission is charged.

This work is published by Samuel French, an imprint of Concord Theatricals Ltd.

The Professional Rights in this play are controlled by Eric Glass Ltd, 25 Ladbroke Cresent, London W11 1PS.

No one shall make any changes in this title for the purpose of production. No part of this book may be reproduced, stored in a retrieval system, scanned, uploaded, or transmitted in any form, by any means, now known or yet to be invented, including mechanical, electronic, digital, photocopying, recording, videotaping, or otherwise, without the prior written permission of the publisher. No one shall share this title, or part of this title, to any social media or file hosting websites.

The moral right of Arnold Ridley to be identified as author of this work has been asserted in accordance with Section 77 of the Copyright, Designs and Patents Act 1988.

USE OF COPYRIGHTED MUSIC

A licence issued by Concord Theatricals to perform this play does not include permission to use the incidental music specified in this publication. In the United Kingdom: Where the place of performance is already licensed by the PERFORMING RIGHT SOCIETY (PRS) a return of the music used must be made to them. If the place of performance is not so licensed then application should be made to PRS for Music (www.prsformusic.com). A separate and additional licence from PHONOGRAPHIC PERFORMANCE LTD (www.ppluk.com) may be needed whenever commercial recordings are used. Outside the United Kingdom: Please contact the appropriate music licensing authority in your territory for the rights to any incidental music.

USE OF COPYRIGHTED THIRD-PARTY MATERIALS

Licensees are solely responsible for obtaining formal written permission from copyright owners to use copyrighted third-party materials (e.g., artworks, logos) in the performance of this play and are strongly cautioned to do so. If no such permission is obtained by the licensee, then the licensee must use only original materials that the licensee owns and controls. Licensees are solely responsible and liable for clearances of all third-party copyrighted materials, and shall indemnify the copyright owners of the play(s) and their licensing agent, Concord Theatricals Ltd., against any costs, expenses, losses and liabilities arising from the use of such copyrighted third-party materials by licensees.

IMPORTANT BILLING AND CREDIT REQUIREMENTS

If you have obtained performance rights to this title, please refer to your licensing agreement for important billing and credit requirements.

COPYRIGHT 1954

CHARACTERS

RODNEY MORCAMBE, a retired business man (aged 65)
AGATHA MORCAMBE, his second wife (aged 40)
PHYLISS MORCAMBE, their daughter (aged 16)
DEREK MORCAMBE, Rodney's son. A solicitor (aged 30)
ELIZABETH BOLTON, Rodney's sister. A widow (aged 55)
LADY SEATON-CLOWES, a local celebrity (aged 50)
LAVINIA, a maidservant (aged 25)

The action of the play takes place in a room in Rodney Morcambe's house in the South-East England provincial town of Lessington during the early part of a November evening.

(Approximate playing time—35 minutes.)

Room Plan

- FIREPLACE (with BELL PUSH)
- LOG BOX
- ARMCHAIR
- TABLE
- CAKE STAND
- SETTEE
- CURTAINED WINDOW
- STANDARD LAMP
- BOOKCASES
- TABLE
- DOOR TO HALL
- STOOL
- DESK
- DOOR TO STUDY

GERANIUM

There is nothing remarkable, architecturally or otherwise, about the lounge in RODNEY MORCAMBE's *house in the small provincial town of Lessington, situated about thirty miles south-east of London. The room (in common with the remainder of the detached villa) is typical of the successful business man who has invested wisely and retired in comfortable circumstances. The furniture is solid and the whole atmosphere is one of good taste. There is a fireplace* R. *and above this a bookcase. The back wall, sloping up a little, contains a french window (not seen) leading into the garden. To the left of this there is a standard lamp and another recessed bookcase. The main door to the room, which leads to the hall, is up* L. *Another wall slopes down from it, and (down* L.) *is another and smaller door leading to* RODNEY's *private study. Before the fire, there is a comfortable chintz-covered settee and, below it, a log box. Upstage of the fire is a large armchair and there is a small table* L.C. *with surrounding chairs. Between the two doors (*L.*) stands a desk with the usual desk stool. The few pictures on the wall are modern and there are also a number of photographs, both of individuals and groups, on the mantelpiece and the desk. Also on the mantelpiece stands a clock of the type that suggests a presentation. Conspicuous upon the table (*L.C.*) is a small geranium in a fancy pot decorated with frilled paper. This geranium has a rather pathetic air and at once strikes the attention by the fact that it appears rather out of place in its rather ornate surroundings. There are various magazines scattered around the room, which appears not only comfortable but also well used by the entire family.*

When the curtain rises, it is about four o'clock on a Saturday afternoon in late November. The chintz curtains over the french window have been drawn, the lights are on and the fire burns brightly.

RODNEY MORCAMBE *and his second wife,* AGATHA, *are finishing tea served from another small table before the fire. A tea trolley and a small three-tier cake stand are near by.* RODNEY MORCAMBE *sits in the armchair above the fire and* AGATHA *at the top end of the settee.* RODNEY *is a good-looking and well-preserved man of about sixty-five, dressed in a tweed suit of good taste. Cup in one hand and with his plate on the arm of his chair, he is holding a book in the other, which he reads to the exclusion of his wife's company.* AGATHA, *a pretty but rather vague woman of forty, is staring absently into the fire. She is dressed expensively but lacks the air of self-confidence a woman usually gains by the wearing of good clothes.*

For a moment there is silence, and then RODNEY, *who has finished his book, closes it and drops it on the floor beside him, on his left, with a short grunt. This has the effect of arousing* AGATHA *from her day-dream.*

AGATHA (*quietly, but pleasantly*). More tea, dear?

RODNEY. Eh? Oh yes—thanks.

(*He holds out his cup towards her but not near enough for her to reach without getting up to take it, which she does.*)

Pretty poor brew.

AGATHA (*busy with the cup*). Is it, dear? It's quite fresh. I only bought it this morning and it's the same we always have.

RODNEY. I asked you to try the stuff they gave us at the Medways the other day. Let me see, what was it called—er—er? (*He snaps his fingers while trying to remember.*) Anyway, you wrote it down, didn't you?

AGATHA. Yes, dear, but I lost the bit of paper. I'm so sorry.

RODNEY (*slightly irritated*). Oh it doesn't matter.

AGATHA. But it does, dear. (*Rising and giving* RODNEY *his cup again.*) I meant to ring Joan Medway and ask her, but I forgot. I'll phone her in the morning. (*Adds.*) But I expect it's rather expensive.

RODNEY (*pompously*). Nothing is expensive if it's what you really want.

AGATHA. No, dear. (*Adds.*) If you can afford to pay for it.

RODNEY. Exactly. (*As the clock on the mantelpiece commences to strike five.*) Good heavens! What *is* that girl doing?

AGATHA. Lavinia, dear?

RODNEY. Good God, no! Since when have I taken to calling our parlourmaid "the girl", may I ask?

AGATHA (*obviously crushed*). I'm sorry, Rodney.

RODNEY. I *do* wish you'd be more careful in avoiding the use of those common expressions. "Girl" indeed!

AGATHA. But Rodney—it wasn't *I* who said——

RODNEY (*interrupting*). I was referring to our daughter Phyliss. Why is she so late for tea?

AGATHA. She's having a bath, dear. She's been playing hockey this afternoon.

RODNEY. Oh! I'm not sure I approve of all this hockey nonsense.

AGATHA. Nor do I entirely, Rodney. I'm always afraid she may get hurt.

RODNEY. It's not that. It's that I don't care much for her barging about with all these tradesmen and scholarship types. She ought to have gone to a proper boarding school.

AGATHA. But I didn't like the idea of her being away from home and——

RODNEY. And I gave in to you. Silly of me.

AGATHA. But at a boarding school she would still have played hockey. I did when I was a girl.

RODNEY. You weren't *at* a boarding school.

AGATHA. No. But I played hockey. Once I was chosen for the first team.

RODNEY (*surprised*). You?

AGATHA. There was an epidemic of chicken-pox at the time and they were very short.

RODNEY. Oh I see.

AGATHA (*sadly*). But on the morning of the match I got it, too; so I didn't play after all.

RODNEY (*rising and casually feeling for his pipe*). Just as well, I should imagine.

AGATHA. I expect so. I was never very good at games. (*Picks up the volume* RODNEY *has thrown down.*) Was it an interesting book, dear?

RODNEY. Not particularly. All about the Everest expedition.

AGATHA (*turning the pages*). I think I'll read it myself before it goes back to the library.

RODNEY. Too scientific. (*Searching for matches on the mantelpiece.*) You wouldn't understand it.

AGATHA. Perhaps not, dear. (*Rises and puts the book on the table* L.C.) Oh dear! The geranium!

RODNEY. Eh?

AGATHA (*picking up the pot with care*). I'm sure it ought not to be in this warm room. Fires are so bad for plants, aren't they?

RODNEY (*lighting his pipe*). Only *gas* fires. *Coal* fires do no harm.

AGATHA. Oh I see. (*Puts down the pot.*) It would be terrible if it died.

RODNEY. It will die if you go on watering it every hour or so. (*Sits again.*)

AGATHA. But I thought—(*Adds.*) I expect you're right, dear.

(*The door up* L. *is thrown open and* PHYLISS MORCAMBE *comes hurrying in. She is a pretty and attractive girl of sixteen, full of life and inclined to be noisy.*)

PHYLISS (*cheerfully*). Hello, Mummy! Still gloating over the trophy? (*Crosses to* RODNEY *and kisses him lightly.*) Good evening, Daddy. Sorry if I'm late.

RODNEY (*with slight reproof*). It's gone five, you know, Phyliss.

PHYLISS. I know. But I had a long soak in the hot bath. I've got a bruise on my bottom.

RODNEY. Really! Phyliss!

PHYLISS. Well, on my— (*She is about to use an even more vulgar word but recovers herself.*)—on my *rump* then. (*Takes up a position back to fire and tenderly rubs the injured portion of her anatomy.*)

AGATHA (*crossing to pour tea*). Were you hit by the ball, dear?

PHYLISS. Of course not, Mother. Never turn your back on the foe. One of those All Saints cows charged me into the goal posts. If their beastly games mistress hadn't been umpiring it would have been a penalty bully. They always were a foul lot of ticks at All Saints. But I got her all right later on though; clocked her one on the ankle during a scrimmage and she had to go off the field.

RODNEY. It sounds disgracefully unladylike to me.

PHYLISS. But awful fun, Daddy. (*With satisfaction.*) Grand!

RODNEY. I take it you won the match, then?

PHYLISS. No. They beat us four to three. (*Cheerfully.*) But we play them again next term; on our ground, too. We'll bash hell out of the trollops. You just see.

RODNEY. Really, Phyliss! I cannot and will not allow you to use such expressions——

PHYLISS (*easily*). Sorry, Daddy. (*Moves to the tea trolley and lifts the lid from a silver dish.*) What! No crumpets!

AGATHA (*handing her a cup of tea*). But surely—— (*Looks at the empty dish.*) Oh, I expect Lavinia has forgotten to bring them in. Just touch the bell, Rodney, will you? (*Adds quickly.*) No, don't move. (*Crosses up to his chair and presses the bell close to it.*)

PHYLISS. Didn't you have any, then? (*To* AGATHA.) I thought you adored them.

AGATHA. Your father thinks they are bad for the digestion, dear.

PHYLISS. That's only because he doesn't take enough exercise. (*To* RODNEY.) You're getting fat, Daddy.

AGATHA (*shocked*). He's not in the least bit fat, Phyliss.

PHYLISS (*cheerfully*). But he will get fat if he slacks about so much. (*Adds.*) Then they won't elect him mayor next year, and that would be an awful sell after the way he's sweated blood for it, wouldn't it?

RODNEY. I'll have you know, Phyliss, that I have done no such thing. The suggestion that I should be mayor came as a complete surprise to me.

PHYLISS. Sez you! (*Adds quickly.*) I say! If you're the mayor, Mummy will be mayoress, won't she? I can't sort of imagine Mummy as the mayoress. (*To* AGATHA.) Hope you won't make a muck of it, Mummy darling: you know, get mixed up between the Licensed Victuallers and the Total Abstinence League.

RODNEY. I'm sure your mother will carry out her duties to the best of her ability.

(LAVINIA *enters up* L. *She is a trim maid in cap and apron.*)

LAVINIA (*to* AGATHA). You rang, m'am?

AGATHA (*crossing and meeting* LAVINIA *above table*). Yes, Lavinia. You forgot to bring in the crumpets.

LAVINIA. There aren't any, m'am.

PHYLISS. What!

AGATHA. But surely, Lavinia . . . Do you mean the baker forgot to send them?

LAVINIA. He said none were ordered, m'am. I asked him particular, m'am, because I know you usually have crumpets the days Miss Phyliss plays croquet.

PHYLISS (*indignantly*). Hockey, Lavinia! I wouldn't be seen dead playing croquet!

AGATHA. He must have made a mistake, Lavinia. I ordered them especially when I called at Crossmans this morning. (*Adds doubtfully.*) At least I think I did.

LAVINIA. He said you didn't, m'am.

PHYLISS. You must have forgot, Mummy! What a beastly swiz!

AGATHA (*coming back to behind settee*). I'm terribly sorry, dear.
PHYLISS (*cheering up*). Never mind, Mummy. I'll have cake instead. As a matter of fact I've had one tea already. (*Grabs a large slice of cake from the stand.*)
LAVINIA. Will that be all, m'am?
AGATHA. Yes, thank you, Lavinia.
    (LAVINIA *goes out, and there is a short pause.*)
RODNEY. You really must do something about your memory, Agatha.
PHYLISS. It's the geranium, Daddy, gone to her head.
AGATHA (*suddenly tearful*). I think you're all very unkind about my poor little geranium. (*Turns away towards the table.*)
PHYLISS (*hurrying across the room and putting an arm around her*). I was only fooling, Mummy darling. It's a lovely geranium. It's the finest geranium that ever gerained, and I think it was wonderful of you to win it. (*Adds.*) I bet old Pie-Face will be surprised!
RODNEY. And who, may I inquire, is "Pie-Face"?
PHYLISS. Derek, of course! (*Returns to the fire.*)
AGATHA (*at back of the settee*). I don't think you should refer to your brother like that, Phyliss.
PHYLISS. But he's not my brother, Mummy dear . . . only my half-brother. (*With a glance towards* RODNEY.) And sometimes I think the wrong half, too.
    (RODNEY *looks up sharply, and she hurries on.*)
What time is he expected back?
AGATHA. Not till Monday. Unless he wires.
RODNEY. I understood he was going to wire if he *was* staying at Eastbourne.
AGATHA. Did you, dear? Then I suppose he *isn't* staying. (*Adds.*) Or is he?
PHYLISS. It probably depends on the floosy.
AGATHA (*puzzled*). Floosy, dear?
PHYLISS (*brightly*). That's right. What I mean is this: there's some

kind of mystery about Derek's sudden trip to Eastbourne, isn't there? My surmise is that it's a week-end date with a floosy.

AGATHA (*shocked*). Phyliss!

RODNEY. Really, Agatha, I have no idea from where your daughter's vulgarity of mind comes; certainly not from me.

PHYLISS. Sorry, Daddy! But I don't think there's anything vulgar in going off with a floosy for the week-end. (*Adds.*) Unless, of course, it's a *vulgar* floosy.

RODNEY. And quite apart from the disrespectful way you speak of your brother, let me remind you that Derek is a solicitor by profession . . .

PHYLISS (*interposing*). Only just, Daddy.

RODNEY (*resenting the interruption*). A solicitor by profession and has recently acquired a partnership in a highly respectable firm . . .

PHYLISS. I was only joking. I don't really think Derek has gone off with a floosy. (*Adds.*) He hasn't the guts.

RODNEY (*very indignantly*). Really! (*Turning to* AGATHA.) What they teach girls at this disgusting school I really don't know!

PHYLISS. D'you mean the facts of life lecture, Daddy? Yes, it *was* rather embarrassing.

RODNEY. I'm glad you found it so.

PHYLISS. I mean, having to pretend we didn't know all about it already.

RODNEY (*to* AGATHA). I'm at a loss for words, Agatha, completely!

PHYLISS (*brightly*). Never mind, Daddy. You'll soon find them again.

RODNEY. That a daughter of mine . . . really.

(*Any further discussion on the matter is interrupted by the sudden entrance of* DEREK MORCAMBE. DEREK *is* RODNEY'S *son by his first marriage. Despite his horn-rimmed spectacles, he is a good-looking but slightly pedantic young man of thirty. He wears a well-cut dark suit and appears more than a little pleased with himself.)*

DEREK *(as he enters)*. Good evening.

AGATHA *(turning)*. Why . . . Derek!

DEREK. Good evening, Mother. *(The studied use of the word is noticeable but not pronounced.)* How are you? *(He pecks her cheek.)* Good evening, Father. Evening, Phyl.

PHYLISS. Hello! So she let you down, did she?

DEREK *(surprised)*. Eh? *(Looks at* PHYLISS *very sharply.)*

PHYLISS. The floosy you——*(Catching* RODNEY'S *eye.)* Sorry!

AGATHA. I didn't expect you till Monday, Derek. You said you'd wire, didn't you?

DEREK. If I was *staying*, yes. It wasn't necessary.

AGATHA. Then I expect you'd like some tea. *(Moves a little towards the bell push.)*

DEREK *(stopping her)*. I had tea on the train.

PHYLISS. Lucky for you. No crumpets! *(Seizes another piece of cake.)*

RODNEY. Then I take it that the business that necessitated this trip to Eastbourne has turned out satisfactory. Eh?

DEREK *(with a half smile)*. Entirely.

RODNEY. Of course I didn't ask you what it was . . .

DEREK *(cutting in)*. And if you *had* I shouldn't have told you.

RODNEY *(resenting this a little)*. Of course, I understand that in professional matters a modicum of secrecy has to be preserved. All the same . . .

DEREK *(again cutting in)*. It wasn't a professional matter, Father. The—er—business—that took me to Eastbourne was entirely private.

PHYLISS. There you are! I told you so.

DEREK *(coldly)*. I beg your pardon.

PHYLISS. I said you'd gone to keep a date with a wench.

DEREK *(R. centre)*. As a matter of fact, Phyl, and allowing for your strip cartoon mind, you are surprisingly near the truth.

Rodney (*surprised*). What!
Derek (*easily*). I went to Eastbourne to see Mrs. Redvers Montgomery.
Phyliss (*surprised at last*). Mrs. Redvers Montgomery? But she's not a wench. Sixty if she's a day.
Derek. Kindly do not interrupt. (*To* Rodney *and* Agatha.) I went to Eastbourne to see Mrs. Redvers Montgomery and ask her consent to my marriage to her daughter Celia.
Agatha (*coming to* L. *of table*). Derek!
Phyliss. Crikey Harry!
Rodney. My dear Derek! I had no idea of this!
Derek (*calmly*). No. (*Sitting on back of settee.*) On Wednesday night at the Territorial Ball I asked Celia to be my wife and she did me the honour of accepting me—subject to her mother's approval of the engagement. As you are aware, her father died in March.
Rodney. But, my dear boy, you didn't say a word . . .
Derek. I saw no point in mentioning the matter until it was finally settled.
Phyliss. You mean the old trout might have put the bar up to the whole thing?
Derek (*coldly*). Not at all. And I should be obliged if you would restrain yourself from referring to my prospective mother-in-law as an old trout.
Agatha. Mother-in-law? Then you mean . . .?
Derek. Mrs. Redvers Montgomery has given her full consent to the engagement. It struck me that there might be minor difficulties to be overcome, Celia being an only child, and that was why I entertained the possibility of having to remain in Eastbourne over the week-end. (*Rising.*) But, as a matter of fact . . .
Phyliss. She swept you to her bosom with a cry of delight.
Derek (*ignoring this*). She raised no obstacle whatever—even agreed to the wedding taking place in April.

AGATHA. Derek! How splendid! (*Goes to him and kisses him warmly.*)
DEREK. Thank you, Mother.
PHYLISS (*rushing and kissing him*). Good for you, Derek! And I hope you'll have dozens of brats.
AGATHA. Phyliss!
PHYLISS (*crossing in front of them to* L.). Why not, Mummy? I've always wanted to be an aunt. (*Remembering.*) Of course I shall only be a half-aunt really, I suppose. (*To* DEREK.) Shall I be a half-aunt or half an aunt? You're a solicitor and ought to know.
DEREK. I suggest we consider the matter at a later and more appropriate date. (*Turns to* RODNEY.) Well, Father?
RODNEY (*shaking his hand*). My dear Derek, I congratulate you, of course, but—er——(*He breaks off.*)
DEREK (*coldly again*). Well, what, Father?
RODNEY (*back to fire*). Well, I do think you might have told me before.
DEREK. Why? Surely you don't disapprove?
RODNEY. Oh no. Redvers Montgomery was a great friend of mine and the senior partner in your firm. Celia is a most charming girl . . .
PHYLISS. And positively filthy with lucre.
RODNEY. That has nothing to do with it, Phyliss. (*To* DEREK.) Although I admit a little financial backing will be useful to you in the early years of your marriage. It's just that I think I ought to have been consulted.
DEREK. I'm sorry, Father. I had no intention of hurting your feelings.
RODNEY (*magnanimously*). Then we'll say no more about it. (*Once more shakes* DEREK *by the hand.*) Well, well, well!
PHYLISS. Of course I'll be a bridesmaid. I shall wear pink with an orange and green hat with osprey plumes. Gosh! What a year next year is going to be! Daddy mayor, Mummy

mayoress, Derek leading character in a slap-up wedding! It only needs Aunt Lizzie to grab an O.B.E. for good works to put the tin hat on it.

DEREK. Talking about Aunt Elizabeth, I saw her just now.

RODNEY. Oh? When?

DEREK. When I was in the taxi on the way from the station. She was coming up Mulberry Avenue in her usual determined way. I tried to get the driver to stop, but he didn't hear me until it was too late.

PHYLISS. Hell's bells! I hope she's not coming here! (*Reflectively.*) Mulberry Avenue. Half a mile at her Brigade of Guards' rate of marching. (*Calculating.*) Well, we'll soon know if the worst is going to happen.

AGATHA. I'm sure your aunt means well, Phyliss.

PHYLISS. That's the worst part of it. (*Sits on desk stool.*)

DEREK (*changing the subject*). Nothing exciting happened while I've been away, I suppose?

RODNEY. I don't think so, Derek.

PHYLISS. Daddy darling! How can you say such a thing. (*To DEREK.*) Something most tremendously exciting has happened. (*Indicates the geranium with a dramatic gesture.*) Look!

DEREK (*turning and viewing the pot with obvious distaste*). Good heavens! What's this?

PHYLISS. It's a geranium, my sweet idiot. Don't they teach botany at the Law Society? Mummy won it yesterday.

DEREK (*surprised*). Won it? How?

PHYLISS. At the St. Jude's whist drive.

DEREK. Oh, I see. Booby prize, eh?

AGATHA (*with sudden spirit*). Certainly not! It was the first prize and I think it's lovely!

DEREK (*taken aback a little*). I beg your pardon.

AGATHA (*above table*). Whatever makes you think it was the booby prize, Derek?

RODNEY. Probably because Derek knows as well as I do

that you're the world's worst cards player, my dear Agatha.

DEREK (*trying to cover up his error*). I didn't mean that exactly. After all, whist is about the easiest game ever invented . . .

PHYLISS. Not when Mummy plays it. (*With sudden contrition.*) Sorry, Mummy darling! (*Takes* AGATHA's *arm.*)

AGATHA. It's all right, dear. I'm not very good, I admit.

DEREK. What I really meant was that it seems rather a poor specimen, for a first prize, that is. It can't have cost more than one-and-six, can it?

AGATHA. It's only a small whist drive at St. Jude's, Derek; not more than six tables at the most.

PHYLISS. Anyway, Mummy won it. Didn't you, Mummy?

AGATHA. Yes, I did win it. And I'm very proud of it.

PHYLISS. And so am I, Mummy. We'll buy some liquid manure for it and then perhaps it will grow.

RODNEY. Not in that terrible pot, I trust.

(*The door up* L. *opens and* LAVINIA *appears.*)

Yes, Lavinia?

LAVINIA. Mrs. Bolton has called, sir.

PHYLISS (*jumping up*). I knew it. The worst has happened.

RODNEY. Be quiet, Phyliss. (*To* LAVINIA.) Show my sister in, please, Lavinia.

LAVINIA. Yes, sir. (*Exit.*)

RODNEY (*to* PHYLISS). I think the least you might do is to try and behave like a lady before the servants.

PHYLISS (*still unrepentant*). We've only one servant, Daddy.

AGATHA. No, dear. You're forgetting Mrs. Playfair.

PHYLISS. Oh, I don't count her as a servant, Mummy darling. She says she only comes to oblige.

(LAVINIA *opens the door to admit* MRS. ELIZABETH BOLTON *and then goes out.* ELIZABETH BOLTON, *who is* RODNEY's *sister, is indeed a formidable figure. She is a woman of fifty-five, much given to tweeds, heavy shoes, walking sticks and good works. Having driven her husband to an early grave, she now attempts to force her authority on the rest of the world; her relations in particular.*)

AGATHA (*as* ELIZABETH *enters*). Good evening, Elizabeth. How nice to see you!

ELIZABETH (*gruffly*). Evening. (*Almost ignoring* AGATHA, *she crosses towards* RODNEY.) Good evening, Rodney.

RODNEY. How are you, Elizabeth?

ELIZABETH. Quite well, of course, thank you. (*Curtly, to* PHYLISS.) Good evening, Phyliss. Don't say *you're* pleased to see me because I know you're not!

PHYLISS. Oh, Aunty Lizzie, how can you think such a thing?

ELIZABETH (*above settee*). Because it's true. I was told what you said about me to that Maggie Travers girl the other day. And don't call me Aunt Lizzie.

PHYLISS. I'm sorry, Aunt Liz— (*Hastily.*) Aunt Elizabeth. I forgot.

ELIZABETH. Then don't forget. (*To* DEREK.) I've seen you before. You went crashing past me in a taxi coming up Mulberry Avenue.

DEREK. I know. I tried to get the driver to stop and give you a lift, but . . .

ELIZABETH (*interrupting him*). Prefer to walk. Good for the body and stimulates the mind. (*To* RODNEY.) You ought to walk more, Rodney. You're going to seed in an appalling way. (*Swinging back to* DEREK.) Suppose I must congratulate you on your engagement.

DEREK (*astonished*). But, heavens above, who told you about it? It's a complete secret.

ELIZABETH. Heard about it last night. (*Comes round and sits on settee.*) Well, I suppose you might have done worse. A stick-in-the-mud like you mustn't expect too much. Celia Montgomery is a bit of a nit-wit, but she's pretty enough despite the fact that she has bow legs.

DEREK. Bow legs! I'm sure she hasn't!

ELIZABETH. You can take it from me she has.

PHYLISS. Well, he'll find out after they're married, won't he, Aunty?

ELIZABETH. Don't be disgusting, Phyliss. (*Sweeping on.*) And her father left her seventy-three thousand; in trust, of course.

DEREK. No. Forty-eight thousand.

ELIZABETH. In the will, yes. But he "made-over" twenty-five four years before he died.

DEREK. Did he? I—I didn't know.

ELIZABETH. Well, you do now.

AGATHA (*after a very short pause*). Er—can I get you some tea, Elizabeth? I'm sure . . .

ELIZABETH. I don't take tea, Agatha. One meal a day. A good sensible midday dinner. Coffee and fruit juice in the morning and a cup of Ovaltine with a glass of old port before retiring. That's all anyone needs. (*Suddenly swings around towards the table and glares at the geranium.*) So *there* it is! (*Rises and crosses to table.*)

AGATHA. My geranium, yes. Isn't it pretty?

ELIZABETH. Can't stand geraniums. Never could. There were quite a lot at The Towers when poor Henry bought the place, but I made him root them up. Anyway, flowers in the house are unhealthy.

AGATHA (*anxiously*). You mean they die?

ELIZABETH. I didn't say that. I said they were unhealthy.

AGATHA. Oh. Er—oh, I see.

ELIZABETH. I may as well say straight away that I've come here this evening to see Rodney. On business. Family business and private.

AGATHA. I see. Well, in that case . . . (*She is about to move.*)

RODNEY. We'll go into my study then, Elizabeth. (*He, too, is about to move.*)

AGATHA. No, no. You can't do that, Rodney. There's no fire.

We'll go into the study and you can talk to Elizabeth here. (*Moves towards the door down* L.)

PHYLISS (*protesting*). But I haven't finished my tea yet! (*Comes* C.)

RODNEY. Do as your mother tells you, Phyliss.

PHYLISS (*grumbling*). Oh, all right. (*Grabs yet another piece of cake and crosses to the door which* AGATHA *is holding open.*)

(DEREK *moves to follow.*)

ELIZABETH. You can stay, Derek.

DEREK. But I thought you said . . .

ELIZABETH (*with decision*). I prefer that you stay, Derek.

DEREK. Very well.

(DEREK *crosses and closes the door after* AGATHA *and* PHYLISS *have gone out. He then crosses back above the settee, leaving* ELIZABETH *in the centre of the room staring coldly at the geranium. There is a pause during which* RODNEY *sits again in his chair.*)

RODNEY (*back to fire*). Well, Elizabeth, what's it all about?

ELIZABETH. This, of course. (*Points.*) This geranium!

RODNEY (*surprised*). But, I thought you said you wanted to speak to me on a family matter. Something important.

(*There is a pause, during which* RODNEY *sits again in his chair.*)

ELIZABETH. So I do. (*Strides across and seats herself on the settee.*) You've made a mistake, Rodney. A bad mistake. I told you so at the time, but you preferred to disregard my advice. *Now* you will see that I was right.

RODNEY (*still puzzled*). What mistake?

ELIZABETH. You should never have married Agatha!

RODNEY. Really, Elizabeth. You can't say a thing like that.

ELIZABETH. I can and I do! (*Sits* R. *of table.*) You shouldn't have married again. I don't consider it was right. I'm sure Henry would never have married again if I'd died before him. (*Adds.*) He wouldn't have dared.

RODNEY (*crossing behind settee to* ELIZABETH). But, damn it all, Elizabeth, I was still quite a young man when Marion passed on.

ELIZABETH. You were nearly fifty.
RODNEY. Well, that's still young . . . young enough. Derek was just going away to school. I wanted a home. Poor Marion had been an invalid for several years. I had the right to start my life again.
ELIZABETH. Then you should have chosen a more suitable woman. Agatha had no background; daughter of a tradesman and obliged to earn her own living as a secretary of some sort. Although how she did it beats me, seeing that she hasn't the brain of a rabbit. That's probably why she married a man old enough to be her father.
DEREK (*dropping* D.R.). A very young father, Aunt Elizabeth.
ELIZABETH. Please don't joke, Derek.
DEREK. I'm not joking. Quite apart from Father's feelings, you must remember that in addition to being his wife she is Phyliss's mother, also my stepmother and has always treated me with the utmost kindness.
RODNEY. Really, Elizabeth, I don't see any reason for us to discuss the matter any further.
ELIZABETH. Don't forget the geranium!
RODNEY (*bursting out*). What, in the name of fortune, has the geranium to do with my marriage to Agatha?
ELIZABETH. Quite a bit. (*Rising, she crosses to above the table.*) Have you any idea how Agatha came by this—this plant?
RODNEY. Of course. She won it at St. Jude's whist drive yesterday afternoon.
ELIZABETH. Do you know how she won it?
DEREK. By having the top score, I should surmise.
ELIZABETH. Exactly. Gained by cheating.
         (*For a second there is a pause.*)
RODNEY. My dear Elizabeth, I can only think that you've taken leave of your senses.
DEREK. I've never heard anything so absurd in my life! (*Turns away towards* R.)

ELIZABETH (*quietly but firmly*). The fact remains that Agatha won the geranium by cheating. I heard about it only two hours ago.

RODNEY. Who from?

ELIZABETH. Lady Seaton-Clowes. As you know, she runs the whist drives at St. Jude's and gives the prizes; why, I don't know, but I suppose she likes playing Lady Bountiful and being fawned upon by the rector. Anyway, she organises the whole stupid affair, and after Agatha had gone yesterday Lady Seaton-Clowes discovered that she'd won the first prize by cheating.

RODNEY. Absurd!

ELIZABETH. I can only repeat that it's the truth. What reason would Lady Seaton-Clowes have for telling me a thing like that if it wasn't? I don't suppose she wants a scandal in the parish any more than I want one in the family. Just think of it, Rodney: you, the mayor elect, Agatha the mayoress to be; you, Derek, about to make a most advantageous marriage; and Agatha branded as having cheated at cards. What a story!

DEREK. If it were true, but the whole thing is utter nonsense.

RODNEY. Of course. (*Coming towards* ELIZABETH.) Tell me this, Elizabeth. Why should Agatha cheat at cards to win a miserable little geranium in a horrible pot? The thing isn't worth half-a-crown.

DEREK. About one-and-six I should say.

RODNEY. Exactly. (*To* ELIZABETH.) Agatha isn't hard up. I give her an ample sum for housekeeping and she has a handsome dress allowance as well. If she wanted a geranium she could buy one, and a far better geranium than that pathetic specimen.

DEREK. Quite right, Father. There's no motive whatsoever.

ELIZABETH. I'm not concerned with motives, Derek. I'm only concerned with facts, and Lady Seaton-Clowes says that Agatha won the geranium by cheating.

RODNEY. Has she told anyone else?

ELIZABETH. I don't think so. She came to me first, but she may have done. I don't know.

RODNEY. If she does repeat this ridiculous lie it's a libel. Isn't it, Derek? Slander, I mean.

DEREK. A most serious slander, too, and one deserving of very heavy damages.

ELIZABETH. Well, there it is, and I came to see you at once.

DEREK. You were quite right. (*Crosses down towards the door.*)

RODNEY. Where are you going, Derek?

DEREK (*turning*). To fetch Mother. Will you please leave this to me, Father? Don't forget I'm a lawyer. (*Opens the door and calls off.*) Mother! Will you come in here for a moment, please?

(DEREK *holds the door open as* AGATHA *returns, and closes it behind her.*)

AGATHA (*nervously*). Is anything the matter?

DEREK. In a way, yes. But there's nothing for you to worry about. Please sit down. (*Indicates the settee.*)

AGATHA. Very well, Derek.

(AGATHA *sits down on the edge of the settee.* DEREK *crosses back to the fireplace, removes his spectacles and adopts what he considers to be a suitable Law Courts attitude.*)

DEREK. Now I want you to listen to me very carefully, please, and not get excited.

AGATHA. I'll try, Derek.

DEREK. Aunt Elizabeth has come here this evening because she's heard a very stupid story.

AGATHA. What about?

RODNEY (*behind* R. *end of settee*). Your geranium.

AGATHA. But, who on earth would want to tell a story about my poor little geranium?

ELIZABETH. Lady Seaton-Clowes says you won it by cheating.

AGATHA (*jumping up quickly*). What?

DEREK. Which, of course, is absolutely untrue.

AGATHA. Of course. (*Sits again.*)
DEREK (*triumphantly to* ELIZABETH). There you are, you see.
  (ELIZABETH *contents herself with shrugging her shoulders.*)
AGATHA. I don't think I could cheat even if I wanted to. (*Adds.*) I doubt if I'm clever enough.
RODNEY. Exactly.
ELIZABETH. Lady Seaton-Clowes says you did.
AGATHA (*agitated*). Then I'm sure there must be some mistake. What I mean is that Lady Seaton-Clowes is a most pleasant lady and wouldn't say a terrible thing like that unless it was true.
ELIZABETH. She wouldn't.
AGATHA. I mean, unless she *thought* it was true.
RODNEY. Which it isn't.
AGATHA. No, there's been some silly mistake.
DEREK. It's more than silly, it's a wicked mistake.
AGATHA. Perhaps if I were to go and see Lady Seaton-Clowes . . .
ELIZABETH (*rising*). No need. She'll be here any moment now. I asked her to be good enough to call at five-thirty, and she agreed.
DEREK (*astonished*). She's—coming—here?
  (ELIZABETH *nods.*)
RODNEY (*angrily*). Really, Elizabeth, you take too much upon yourself. To ask this woman who has told this horrible untruth about my wife to my house—to *Agatha's* house . . . (*He becomes too indignant to continue.*)
ELIZABETH. Things to do with the family and the family's honour concern me just as much as they do you, Rodney. Please remember that. By getting Lady Seaton-Clowes here and talking things over in a friendly way we may be able to persuade her to allow the whole matter to be hushed up.
DEREK. It's not going to be hushed up. Lady Seaton-Clowes has perpetrated a slander which affects us all very seriously.

AGATHA. But, perhaps it would be the best thing to do. After all, Derek, it isn't as if the geranium was very valuable or . . .

DEREK (*interrupting her*). My dear Mother, the value of the geranium has nothing to do with it. The point at issue is that you have been accused of a dishonest action. Besides, things like this never *are* hushed up. Stories of this sort always get out in some way or other, especially in a place like Lessington, and the fact that there had been an attempt to hush it up would appear as an admission of guilt.

AGATHA (*sitting on settee*). I only want to do what is best, Derek.

DEREK (*sitting beside* AGATHA). There is only one thing. Lady Seaton-Clowes must withdraw the allegation absolutely. She must withdraw the allegation in a legal document properly witnessed, extend a full apology and bind herself never to repeat the ridiculous story ever again.

ELIZABETH (*above table*). And suppose she won't?

DEREK (*rising and going back to fire*). Then we shall issue a writ for slander and claim heavy damages.

AGATHA. But, that would mean the police court, wouldn't it?

DEREK. A law court, yes.

AGATHA (*nervously*). And I should have to give evidence? (DEREK *nods*.) Oh dear, I don't think I'd make a very good witness.

DEREK. You would only have to speak the truth and stick to it. In any case, the chances of the thing going as far as that are very remote indeed. Leave it to me.

AGATHA. But surely, if it did go before a police court . . .

RODNEY. Law court, Agatha.

AGATHA. Law court then. Surely it would mean pieces in the papers, a bigger scandal than ever.

DEREK. That can't be helped. Your character has been attacked and your reputation must be vindicated, even if it had to go as far as the House of Lords.

AGATHA (*distressed*). Oh dear!

RODNEY (*joining* DEREK *at fire*). Derek's quite right, Agatha. You must see that. It's not only you, it's all of us. I'm to be mayor next year, Derek has just gained a partnership in his firm and there is his marriage to be considered. There is a great deal at stake. The whole thing must be settled once for all and in no uncertain manner.

AGATHA. Yes, I—I suppose so. I'll never go to a whist drive again so long as I live.

ELIZABETH. It would certainly be better if you didn't.

(LAVINIA *enters* L.)

LAVINIA (*to* RODNEY). Lady Seaton-Clowes has called, sir.

RODNEY (*with pretended nonchalance*). Oh yes, Lavinia. Please show Lady Seaton-Clowes in.

LAVINIA. Yes, sir. (*Exit.*)

DEREK (*hastily*). I'm not sure you were wise to do that, Father. It's a matter of proper procedure. To see her here . . .

ELIZABETH. Well, you can't do anything about it now.

DEREK. Then leave the talking to me. (*To* AGATHA.) You'd better not be here. It would be most improper for you to meet her.

AGATHA. I'm sure I don't want to, Derek.

(AGATHA *rises and crosses* L., *but at that moment* LAVINIA *opens the door.*)

LAVINIA. Lady Seaton-Clowes, sir.

DEREK. Damnation!

(LADY SEATON-CLOWES *enters. She is a smallish and pleasant-looking woman of about fifty with nothing at all aggressive about her. She wears dark and sober clothes and appears to be very embarrassed.*)

RODNEY. Oh—er—good evening.

LADY SEATON-CLOWES (*coming* R.C.). Good evening.

RODNEY. You know my son, don't you? And—er—my wife?

LADY SEATON-CLOWES. Of course. (*She returns* DEREK's *frigid bow, but avoids looking at* AGATHA.)

RODNEY. And my sister.

ELIZABETH. Of course she does, Rodney. (*To* LADY SEATON-CLOWES.) Glad you've come.

LADY SEATON-CLOWES (*uneasily*). I'm not sure I was wise to do so, all the same, Mrs. Bolton. In fact I feel it would have been far less embarrassing if I'd declined.

DEREK. Exactly.

LADY SEATON-CLOWES. In that case, perhaps . . . (*She moves a pace towards the door.*)

ELIZABETH. Not at all. My brother agrees with me that this very unpleasant matter must be thrashed out thoroughly, and the sooner the better.

LADY SEATON-CLOWES (*hesitating*). I see.

RODNEY. I—e —it was kind of you to take the trouble to visit us, Lady Seaton-Clowes. Perhaps you'll sit down.

LADY SEATON-CLOWES (*very embarrassed*). Well—I——

DEREK (*to* AGATHA). I think it would be a good idea if you left us, Mother.

AGATHA. Oh yes. So do I. (*She moves towards the door down* L.)

ELIZABETH. Not at all. (*By the table.*) It will only mean going over all the same ground again.

DEREK (*shrugging his shoulders in annoyance*). Oh, very well.

RODNEY (*again indicating the settee*). Please!

(LADY SEATON-CLOWES *sits on the settee.* DEREK *remains by the fireplace, and* RODNEY *sits in his chair again.*

AGATHA *seats herself on the desk stool, and* ELIZABETH *remains in a commanding position by the table* L.C.)

LADY SEATON-CLOWES (*quietly, as she sits*). Thank you.

RODNEY (*after a pause*). Of course, Lady Seaton-Clowes, you are—er—aware of the reason for this—er—meeting? (LADY SEATON-CLOWES *nods slowly.*) It—er—concerns a statement you made this afternoon concerning my wife. (LADY SEATON-CLOWES *nods again.*) I understand that—er—you informed my sister that Agatha—my wife—won the first prize at St. Jude's whist drive yesterday afternoon—that geranium—by some dishonest method—by cheating.

LADY SEATON-CLOWES (*quietly*). That is the substance of what I said, yes.

DEREK. Are you prepared to withdraw?

LADY SEATON-CLOWES. I'm afraid not, Mr. Morcambe.

DEREK. You realise, of course, that, by making that remark, you have committed a very serious slander?

LADY SEATON-CLOWES (*still quietly but quite firmly*). I realise that if what I said was *untrue*, it would be a slander. Unfortunately, it is true.

ELIZABETH (*almost in triumph*). There!

LADY SEATON-CLOWES. I fully appreciate the seriousness of the implication and I can assure you that nothing would have induced me to say what I did to Mrs. Bolton had I not been convinced that it was correct . . .

DEREK. You will have to prove that.

LADY SEATON-CLOWES (*calmly*). I *can* prove it, Mr. Morcambe. The score card which Mrs. Morcambe handed in and which won the first prize is in my possession. (*To* RODNEY.) Please understand that I am not actuated by malice in the slightest degree and I wish most profoundly that the—er—the matter had not come to my notice. Unfortunately, I have my duty to perform.

RODNEY (*rising*). But the whole thing is so silly . . . trivial.

LADY SEATON-CLOWES. Up to a point, yes. But, as my late husband used to say, there can be no degrees of honesty. A person is either honest or dishonest and the extent of the dishonesty is immaterial.

DEREK (*to* RODNEY *and* ELIZABETH). That's what I said just now.

LADY SEATON-CLOWES. I'm glad you agree, Mr. Morcambe. St. Jude's Friday whist drives are, of course, very small functions indeed but, as organiser, it is my duty to see that they are conducted properly. The fact remains that the geranium I now see upon your table belongs legally to some person, some person in reduced circumstances possibly, and who has been robbed of it.

AGATHA (*suddenly jumping up*). No, no, Lady Seaton-Clowes. You see I—— (*She breaks off suddenly and sits again.*)

RODNEY. Yes, Agatha?

AGATHA. Oh, it was nothing. I'm sorry.

RODNEY (*coming to L. of settee*). My wife suggests, Lady Seaton-Clowes, that possibly there has been some mistake . . .

LADY SEATON-CLOWES. I should be only too pleased to admit of that possibility. Unfortunately I cannot. As I have already said, the whole thing came to my notice by sheer mischance. I am not of a prying nature.

ELIZABETH. You said something about a score card, didn't you?

LADY SEATON-CLOWES. Yes. It happened like this. When the whist drive was over and Mrs. Morcambe announced as the winner, I was delighted. To the best of my recollection she had never been successful before during all the time she has come to them. Then, after everyone had gone and I was assisting the caretaker to clear the schoolroom, I remembered that Mrs. Morcambe and myself had been partners in a most unfortunate hand. We had, in fact, scored only one trick. It then struck me that Mrs. Morcambe must have been very lucky in the cards she held afterwards in order to make up so much lost ground. So out of sheer curiosity, and I assure you that it was curiosity alone that prompted my action, I picked up Mrs. Morcambe's card which had been left on one of the tables and looked at it.

DEREK. Well?

LADY SEATON-CLOWES. I found that the hand I'd played with Mrs. Morcambe as my partner, the hand in which we had gained only one trick, had been altered by the addition of another stroke so that it read eleven.

RODNEY. But, but I understood that at whist drives, although I know very little about them, the figures are *written* on the cards as a double check.

LADY SEATON-CLOWES. They *should* be, I admit. But we don't take things very seriously at St. Jude's, you know.

DEREK. You must have mistaken the hand.

LADY SEATON-CLOWES. Impossible, Mr. Morcambe. I remember the hand in question most distinctly. Mrs. Morcambe not only trumped my ace but immediately led back into the suit our opponents were endeavouring to establish. Besides there is my own card on which the score appears correctly.

DEREK. But you've no proof that, even if the score was altered, the alteration was made by my stepmother.

LADY SEATON-CLOWES. Who else would do such a thing?

ELIZABETH. Quite. Who?

RODNEY. Of course you deny having done this, Agatha?

AGATHA. It—it's absurd.

DEREK. Lady Seaton-Clowes, let me repeat my former question. Are you prepared to withdraw this accusation?

LADY SEATON-CLOWES (*gravely*). I'm sorry, but no. If I did I should be guilty of a lie.

RODNEY. Will you guarantee that you will never repeat what you have said regarding my wife's honesty?

LADY SEATON-CLOWES. Not out of malice, I assure you. But, naturally, I must bar Mrs. Morcambe from attending any further whist drives at St. Jude's and if an explanation is demanded of me it would have to be given. I cannot permit myself to be placed in the wrong.

DEREK (*with decision*). Then there's only one thing to be done.

LADY SEATON-CLOWES. Yes?

DEREK. An action for slander.

LADY SEATON-CLOWES. That is entirely your affair, Mr. Morcambe.

DEREK. We shall ask for very heavy damages, you know.

LADY SEATON-CLOWES. Indeed?

DEREK. And the costs might prove even heavier.
LADY SEATON-CLOWES. Costs are usually paid by the losing side. Please don't try to threaten me, Mr. Morcambe. My late husband was a magistrate, you may remember, and I am not so unaware of the law as you appear to imagine. (*Rises.*) And now, if you will excuse me, I will leave. (*Moves towards door* U.L.)
RODNEY (*intercepting her*). Lady Seaton-Clowes, for the last time, do you persist in going on with this?
LADY SEATON-CLOWES. The future lies with you, Mr. Morcambe. If you take legal action against me I shall have no option but to defend myself.
AGATHA (*springing up in a panic*). You can't!
LADY SEATON-CLOWES. I can't defend myself, Mrs. Morcambe? I assure you I can.
AGATHA. I mean that this can't go into the police courts, the law courts I mean. It must be stopped. It must be!
RODNEY. What exactly do you mean, Agatha?
AGATHA. I—I mean that I think I can explain. If I could talk to Lady Seaton-Clowes alone, I think I could explain.
DEREK. That would be most improper.
AGATHA. I can't help that. I want to talk to Lady Seaton-Clowes alone.
ELIZABETH. If you've anything to say you'd better say it straight out.
AGATHA. Not before you; Rodney and Derek perhaps, but not before you, Elizabeth.
ELIZABETH. Why?
AGATHA. Because you frighten me. I know you were against Rodney marrying me. I was frightened of you then and I've been frightened of you ever since.
ELIZABETH (*turning*). Well, Rodney, upon my soul!
RODNEY. I think you'd better leave us, Elizabeth. You'll find Phyliss in my study still.
ELIZABETH. I have no intention of leaving you, Rodney.

RODNEY. This is my house, Elizabeth, and I insist upon being obeyed in it.

ELIZABETH. I—well! (*Hesitates and then strides towards the door down* L.) You'll regret this, all of you! (*She goes out and bangs the door.*)

RODNEY (*after a pause*). Now, Agatha, whatever's the matter?

AGATHA (*crossing slowly towards the fire*). I want to explain. I want to explain to Lady Seaton-Clowes what really happened.

DEREK. I warn you to be careful, Mother. If this goes to law...

AGATHA. It mustn't. It can't!

DEREK. Why not?

AGATHA (*sitting slowly on the settee*). Because, what Lady Seaton-Clowes said is quite true. I did it.

DEREK. What!

AGATHA. I did it. I altered the card. I turned the one into an eleven.

RODNEY. Agatha! In God's name, why?

AGATHA. Because I wanted to win the geranium.

RODNEY. Agatha! Have you taken leave of your senses? Do you expect us to believe that you cheated at cards, made a false entry on your score sheet because you wanted to gain possession of a small geranium? (AGATHA *nods*.) But why?

AGATHA. I've told you, Rodney, because I wanted it.

RODNEY. I'd have bought you a dozen geraniums rather than a thing like this should happen.

AGATHA. I didn't want to be bought one. I didn't want to be *given* one. I wanted to *win* one, *that* one.

(RODNEY *and* DEREK *exchange anxious glances.*)

It's all right, I'm not out of my mind or anything like that.

LADY SEATON-CLOWES (*kindly*). I'm sure you're not, Mrs. Morcambe. (*She sits on the log box facing* AGATHA.) You said you were going to explain to me, didn't you?

AGATHA. I'll try. Yesterday afternoon I was early at the whist drive and I looked at the prizes. I always like looking at the prizes although, as you said just now, I've never won one, in fact I've never won anything, not on my own merits. Well, I saw the geranium was the first prize and I thought how nice it would be if I won it. "Perhaps I shall win to-day," I thought and I tried so hard to concentrate and not make the silly mistakes people tell me I do. I did quite well at first and had good cards; once I had three aces and a king. Then there was the hand when we were partners, Lady Seaton-Clowes, when we did so badly. I could see by your face that I'd made some stupid error but I still don't know what it was. Anyway, we made only one trick and I knew that I couldn't possibly win the geranium after that. I felt quite sad about it and, I dare say you'll think me crazy, I felt that the geranium felt sad about it, too. It looked so pathetic there on the teacher's desk. Just my silly imagination of course but .. . . . Then, afterwards, I did better again and made quite a lot of tricks, more than I've ever made before. And it kept on going through my head: "Just that terrible bad hand; if only that one had been a ten or an eleven." I knew it was wrong of me but I couldn't resist, the temptation was too strong for me.

DEREK. You mean you added another one?

AGATHA. Yes, I never thought it possible that anyone would find out. And you're quite wrong about my robbing anyone, Lady Seaton-Clowes, because I made a special point of finding out who would have won the geranium if I hadn't altered the figure on my card. It was that nice old lady Mrs. Yatesfield. So I went to the florists this morning and bought a geranium and sent it to her anonymously. A much nicer geranium than mine it was, so she hasn't suffered by it. In fact, I thought I'd done no harm to anyone.

RODNEY. But surely you must have realised that it was dishonest in principle?

AGATHA. I do now, but not then. I wanted to win something all on my own so badly. I wanted to surprise you all and I did.

In fact, you were all so surprised it almost spoilt it. You see, Rodney dear, I'm so tired of always being the foolish one. "Poor Agatha", "Poor Mummy who forgets", "Poor Mrs. Morcambe who is so bad at cards". It's been like that all my life, how silly I am and how lucky I've been. (*To* LADY SEATON-CLOWES.) My father was a tradesman in quite a small way and he couldn't afford to send me to the Girls' High School unless I won a scholarship. And of course I didn't. But there was a rich distant cousin somewhere who heard about it and paid the fees. And everyone said how lucky I was. And I was, too! Even though I wasn't very good at things and always at the bottom of the class. Then, after my father died and I had to earn my living, a friend of his gave me a job in his office and everybody said again how lucky it was for me because I was so useless. Then I met Rodney and he was generous enough to ask me to marry him and people said how lucky I was to make such a good match. And how lucky I was that his son—you, Derek—didn't resent having a stepmother. And even when Phyliss was born they said how lucky I was in having a girl because there was a boy in the family already. It's always been like that, you see, nobody ever giving me credit for anything I did myself; not that I deserved it of course. Then, yesterday, I thought I saw my chance, the chance to show that I wasn't *always* a fool. I wanted just one moment when people would congratulate me and think I was clever. But I wasn't even clever enough to cheat and now I've ruined everybody. (*She begins to cry softly.*)

RODNEY (*going to her and sitting beside her*). Agatha, my dear! If only I'd known. Don't cry, Agatha, please.

DEREK. Lady Seaton-Clowes, I apologise. There is nothing more to be said. I'm sure you appreciate that we're entirely at your mercy.

LADY SEATON-CLOWES. I do, Mr. Morcambe. Will you please call your aunt?

DEREK. If you insist.

LADY SEATON-CLOWES. I do insist.

(DEREK *shrugs his shoulders, crosses and opens the door down* L.)

DEREK. Will you please come back, Aunt Elizabeth?

(*After a short pause* ELIZABETH *appears*.)

ELIZABETH. Well? Am I permitted to ask if anything has happened?

LADY SEATON-CLOWES (*rising and crossing to her*). Quite a lot has happened, Mrs. Bolton. Something which has altered the whole aspect of the case. Mrs. Morcambe has been kind enough to give me an explanation which I accept without the slightest reserve.

(DEREK, AGATHA *and* RODNEY *turn in astonishment*.)

I must ask you to forget in its entirety anything I may have said to you this afternoon. I withdraw any allegation I made against Mrs. Morcambe and I ask her to be generous enough to accept my fullest apology. Good evening. (*She goes* U.L. *towards the door and turns*.) And I trust I shall see you at St. Jude's next Friday afternoon, Mrs. Morcambe. Then I shall know that you have forgiven me. Good-bye. (*Exit* U.L.)

ELIZABETH. Well, that *is* a surprise!

DEREK. You speak as if it was an unpleasant one, Aunt.

ELIZABETH. Don't be absurd, of course not. Good night. (*Exit* U.L.)

AGATHA. Rodney! Derek! How could she do such a thing? I didn't believe anyone could be as generous as that.

DEREK (*kindly*). There's an old proverb, Mother, "Circumstances alter cases".

AGATHA. All the same . . .

RODNEY. Never mind, Agatha. Try to forget all about it.

PHYLISS, (*bouncing in from down* L). Hi! What's going on in here, eh? And isn't it about time someone watered that geranium?

QUICK CURTAIN

N.B. *Before any performance of this play can be given, application must first be made to* EVANS BROTHERS LIMITED *for a licence. For full particulars refer to* COPYRIGHT NOTICE *on page 2.*

PROPERTY PLOT

ON TABLE (L.C.)
  A small geranium in a decorated pot.

ON MANTELPIECE
  Clock.
  Tobacco jar.
  Photographs and ornaments.

ON DESK (L.)
  Writing materials.
  Pens and inkstand.
  Photographs.

ON SMALL TABLE BEFORE FIRE
  Teapot, milk and hot-water jugs, cups, saucers, etc.
  Silver crumpet dish with lid.

ON CAKE STAND
  Sliced cake.
  Buns and scones.
  Bread and butter.

PERSONAL PROPS FOR RODNEY
  Book.
  Pipe.
  Matches.

EFFECTS: Clock strikes five.

www.ingramcontent.com/pod-product-compliance
Ingram Content Group UK Ltd.
Pitfield, Milton Keynes, MK11 3LW, UK
UKHW022036040125
453204UK00020B/306